Twenty Pearls of *Wisdom*

A Woman's Guide to Self-Preservation

JASMINE WOMACK

ISBN: 978-0-9906099-0-2 (sc)
ISBN: 978-0-9906099-1-9 (e)

Library of Congress Control Number: 2016910085

Editors: Dr. Joel Boyce & Monica Goings

For more information, please visit www.authorjasminewomack.com

P31 Publishing rev. date: 8/3/2016

This book is dedicated to my beautiful
daughter, Zion. Mommy loves you.

Contents

The Pearls of Your Life-Path and Career Choice

The Pearls of Being Social

Acknowledgements

God has sent many angels in my life during my young adulthood who served as true friends and counselors to me, and who, through prayer and patience, assisted me in developing into the pearl that I am today.

To my family, I thank you from the bottom of my heart. I can never repay you for the constant love and support that you have shown me and I hope that I can love as unselfishly as you love me.

To my sister, Jessica, you are the absolute best sister that anyone can have. Thank you for being who you are.

To my brothers Derek and Emanuel, I am proud of the men that you are becoming. I love you dearly.

To Chasity, I never knew that meeting in college would result in a lifetime friendship. You are a wonderful friend with a beautiful soul. I love you and I value what we share.

To my spiritual family, Prophet Dexter, Yvette, Stephanie, Tameka, Suzanne, and the pastors at Ark of Salvation Ministries words will never be enough to express the gratitude and appreciation for what you have done for me. You all give to others effortlessly and I pray that you all are blessed exceedingly, abundantly, and to the overflow to where no man can ever think or imagine. I love you all.

To Marina, I owe you big time. I love you and I appreciate your friendship.

To my husband John, you are God's gift to me. Thank you for loving me, growing with me, and being an excellent father, husband, and awesome example of a man to our children. I love you.

To my four children, you all are a million rays of sunshine. I am blessed to have you in my life.

To my book coaches Lakia Brandenburg and Kantis Simmons, thank you for your time, encouragement, and expertise. To my students, thank you for being a voice of confirmation for me and a continued inspiration. Although students attend school to learn from teachers, teachers definitely learn from their students as well.

To all women in their young womanhood, I thank you for being who you are. It is my prayer that the words in this book can plant a seed that may inspire and encourage you to live wisely and make focused decisions so that you may live a happy, fulfilled life.

Foreword

"Next to Sound Judgment, diamonds and pearls
are the rarest things in the world..."
Jean de la Bruyere

I t is refreshing, Jasmine, to partner with you heeding the clarion call
of responsibility commissioned by the Word of God in Titus 2:3-5:

> "Likewise teach the older women to be reverent in the way
> they live, not to be slanderers or addicts to much wine but
> to teach what is good. Then they can urge the younger
> women to love their husbands and children, to be self
> controlled and pure, to be busy at home and to be kind and
> to be subject to their husbands, so that no one will malign
> the Word of God."

It is our responsibility as mentors and Sage Connectors to speak
to women, both young and old. We are to change their carnal mind
sets and cancel the Devil's plans to tear the fabric of our gender down
with ignorance and resistance. Our gender was created as a "help
meet" according to the wonderful Word of God. However, these
words have been abused over the years, which created a resistance
movement by women. This resistance started when we realized that
we are second to none and should not be treated as a foot stool.

Within the truth of these words, a misunderstanding occurred: being a foot stool was confused with being a stepping stone. We are not to be second because this is not a competition but it is a divine partnership. We are to work together. We are to help and aid our fellow sisters AND brothers to a life of success and happiness with the wisdom that is gained from our everyday lessons of life in order to propel ourselves and others. This collaboration between Jasmine, these pages, and the wisdom that is within her are the stepping stones to developing the internal fortitude to dive for our pearls. We need the lung capacity to dive for these Twenty Pearls desired. These words are like resuscitation to the lungs for deeper diving and better use of the skills needed to create our strand of pearls as jewelry to be worn with honor.

My mother is a woman with roots from the 20th Century. These chapters are the cornerstones of her core beliefs that were taught to me in the 1980s. Jasmine has taken these same beliefs and transformed them for today's vernacular. Raised as a preacher's kid, there was no choice in participating in Sunday's activities. Either you went to church or YOU WENT TO CHURCH. In today's times, so many parents are busy in the hustle and bustle of everyday living that the weekends become the outlet for release and pleasure. This pleasure seeking can dim the decision making ability that we know. Sunday morning worship has been replaced with a television church service and a bowl of cereal. This is a consequence for the parent(s) to recover from a night of fun and compulsory behavior. Not only do weekends have no real spiritual direction, but daily decisions have been convoluted or twisted as well. Media outlets and the internet have become the babysitters of the modern day. It is about time someone with an abundance of wisdom attempted to reach out and give thoughtful, intentional direction to our young ladies of the 21st Century.

Having known Jasmine for a number of years and watching her blossom into the beautiful and motivated author she has become, my honor and obligation as a minister take a second seat to the outstanding message that is within these pages. Being a mother of 7 and married for almost 20 years, these chapters capture the essence of my words as if I penned them myself. This is not just a tool for your family; it is a prerequisite to womanhood.

Pearls have so many connotations. They are the jewelry coveted by many women young and old to adorn the neck as jewelry. Pearls are also the "coined" name for the beautiful teeth that are displayed in our mouths. With both associations, pearls are to be a beautification for the person bearing them. With these Twenty Pearls currently in your hand, allow them to be stationary like teeth so that the words that come out of your mouth will shape your world and the world of others around with competence and dominion. May the results from the wisdom that will come from *Twenty Pearls of Wisdom: A Woman's Guide to Self-Preservation* allow men to see your good works and glorify God which is in heaven that you may be like a pearl necklace in the eyes of God.

Peace and Blessings!
Min. Stephanie Bronner

Preface

Chocolate, vanilla, strawberry, butter pecan…my mouth watered as I perused the selection of ice cream flavors at the local Morelli's Ice Cream Parlor. Luckily, I wouldn't have to take a wild guess as the employees informed me that prior to making a final selection, I could sample any flavor that I wanted. The store employee was patient with me as I took my time savoring each delectable flavor, as its creamy and cold texture filled my palate and made my taste buds explode. Right when I thought I'd made my choice, I noticed an adjacent cooler with interesting flavors such as ginger lavender, coffee fudge brownie, dark chocolate chili and krispy kreamier. OMG, krispy kreamier icecream?! Like my beloved southern doughnut shop Krispy Kreme?! My curiosity was roused. I absolutely HAD to try it. I know the excitement that many people get when they see the "Hot Now" sign on at Krispy Kreme…people rush to get the hot and fresh doughnuts because they are so good and sweet that they literally melt in your mouth. The store clerk continued to stare at me as I stared at her and slowly placed the Krispy Kreme ice cream-covered spoon into my mouth, and…and…

I was disappointed. It was disgusting and way too sweet. The ice-cream tasted nothing like I hoped it would. I decided to go ahead and sample the ginger lavender and dark chocolate chili ice cream also. Finally, I settled on butter pecan, a traditional southern favorite.

I thanked the clerk and exited the shop while enjoying my ice cream and simultaneously wondering why I had wasted so much time when I ended up getting the same ice-cream flavor as always.

I'd like to compare life to that ice cream shop. We have a plethora of choices at our fingertips and so many experiences to have. We can take our time and think about our choices before we decide to move forward on our decision. However, depending on the quality of our choices, we can make the best of our time or we can waste our time, as our choices always have consequences. Those consequences can be good or bad and can determine the quality of our lives.

During my twenties, I selected ice cream flavors that didn't sit well with my palate. I made many choices that sent me down a less-than-favorable path in life. My twenties were filled with many ups and downs, but there were more downs than ups. Although I graduated Magna Cum Laude from college, I struggled greatly during the transition from college to my career. My love life throughout my twenties was filled with disappointment, heartache, and tears, with failed relationship after relationship, and my twenties culminated in a painful divorce after barely a year of marriage.

I purchased my first home, a townhouse, in a quiet neighborhood. I also purchased my first vehicle, which was my dream car: a black convertible BMW with crimson interior and chrome rims. However, I was living on a novice teacher's salary, had student loan and credit card debt, and had to take occasionally take on part-time jobs to try to pay bills and make ends meet.

The twenties are a time of exploration. With an exploring spirit, I decided to quit my job teaching and start a transportation business without conducting the necessary amount of prior research. I was glad to be my own boss, but I had to split the profits from the business with my business partner, and my profits fluctuated depending on the amount of business we took. Due to unforeseen events and the resulting decrease of income, I ended the business and endured minor financial loss and setbacks due to its failure.

By the time I reached my late twenties, I found myself repeating clichés that I grew up hearing the old folks saying, such as "If I knew then what I know now", regretting many of the reckless decisions that I had made. I silently wished that I had made better use of my time and that the decisions I made during that time period in my life were more thoughtful and wise because I would have avoided much of the worry and distress that I experienced.

I spent my twenties trying to get ahead by doing things the way that I thought they should be done. Needless to say, I now understand that I wasted much of my time and energy pursuing things and people that were not for me. Not to mention, I limited myself and I made poor financial decisions that left me suffocating in a sea of debt.

Although painful, these experiences left me with valuable lessons which I refer to as pearls.

Twenty Pearls of Wisdom: A Young Woman's Guide to Self-Preservation is my love letter to young women. Within these pages, I share with you twenty of the most important lessons that I learned between the ages of eighteen and twenty-nine. Unfortunately, I learned most of these lessons the hard way: through experience. As women, it is important to know the power that we have. It is important to realize our worth, our value, and the impact that the decisions that we make within a split second can have on our current and future lives.

Instead of gaining maturity through the difficult lessons of hardship, my hope is that the words, insight, and wisdom contained in *Twenty Pearls* provides you with the inspiration and encouragement to help you make wise and calculated decisions the first time around, so that you can be empowered to create a wonderful and happy life. Enjoy!

The Pearls of
Self-Preservation

Pearl

Create and Maintain a Spiritual Foundation

I t is of no irony nor coincidence that the first pearl involves creating a spiritual foundation. The very first thing that I strongly recommend you to do is to put God as the head of your life. Putting God in the forefront of your life and allowing Him to take lead does not necessarily mean that you must be in church two to three days a week, or standing and shouting when the preacher delivers a Word that seems like it was meant just for you. It means that you should put effort into having a personal relationship with the Creator.

What does a personal relationship with God look like? Contrary to what you may believe, it is quite simple. A personal relationship with God is created by taking time out to pray and study the Word every day. Whether you devote five minutes or fifty minutes; what matters is that you set aside a time to commune with God, learn more about Him (through reading the Word), and develop a relationship with him through prayer and meditation.

When I was in college, I stopped attending church. I actually went to the opposite end of the spectrum and joined a quasi-cult! Following graduation, I became a devout practitioner of an African divination-nature-based spiritual system where we would get "readings" to determine what we should do regarding certain situations. It was during all of these years of being in "the wilderness" as I call it, that I went through the most personal, emotional, and financial turmoil in my life. Regardless of how "knowledgeable" or "cultural" I became, my spirit was suffering. I had a huge void-a deep hole inside my heart -and in my soul. I was looking to many things and people to fill that void.

I was single and making very poor choices when it came to many areas of my life. I was college-educated, working a professional salaried job and a part-time job to make extra pocket money and was still broke. I purchased my first home, drove a convertible luxury car, shopped when I wanted, had the latest technological gadgets, however I was still unhappy and empty. I even started a lucrative business that made a decent amount of money within its first year, but due to unexpected expenses created by employees, I had to shut my business down.

Working wasn't filling the void. Dating wasn't filling the void. Reading wasn't filling the void. Neither was shopping, my entrepreneurial ventures, nor were all of the new-world "spiritual" teachings that I was learning about and incorporating into my life filling the void. As a matter of fact, virtually everything that I put my hands to, failed. The only thing that I was able to keep consistently and do well at, was my job. I knew that something had to change.

At some point, you realize that what you are doing isn't working the way that you are doing it. You can have every excuse and point your finger at this person or that circumstance, but you are the common denominator, and you are the single repeating factor that is included in each situation. When you literally get tired of being sick and tired, you realize that you need to make a change.

For myself and for many people, that change begins with prioritizing and creating a stable spiritual foundation.

The first change I made was to simply begin reading the Bible. It had been years since I'd read it, and I didn't know where to begin. I'd always liked the Book of Proverbs, so I decided to start there. Making that decision was the beginning of the rest of my life.

As I was reading Proverbs, I began to look for a church home where I could grow more in the Word and be around other believers. The only problem was that I didn't trust pastors and I felt like many of them were crooks. I didn't trust pastors because I had experienced more pastors shouting, hooping and hollering and putting on a show for people and not really teaching the congregation spiritual and Biblical principles to help them deal with and address the many challenges of life. Additionally, I had grown up observing friends and family members who were scraping money to pay the light bill, tithe to the church and give love offerings to pastors who then turned and flaunted their wealth by driving expensive foreign cars and bragging about their businesses.

However, I had faith that there were some honest preachers who were serious about true spiritual teaching, and I decided to begin attending church via online satellite. I started by looking up some churches that I had heard on the local radio or seen on T.V. My mother recommended a website to me where the pastors put all of their sermons online for free for anyone who wanted to listen, and after a year of her urging me, I finally decided to check it out.

I saw so many sermon titles that interested me. In one sermon, the pastor talked about how he was a scientist and although he grew up in a church-oriented home, he had a hard time accepting the existence of God-until he realized that the study of science itself proved God's very existence. He broke the whole thing down as to how he came into this understanding. After listening to that sermon, I was hooked. I wanted to visit the church.

During this time, I was living with a young man who was not my husband. The relationship began to be unfulfilling; however, I remained in the relationship for financial stability. He didn't seem too phased by my new thirst and search for God, but initially, he didn't stop me. It wasn't until I started trying to physically attend church regularly that my efforts would be sabotaged. Every Sunday, something crazy would occur and I would be stuck watching church online. I was so upset.

One day, I was determined to make it to church. I put on a really nice dress and told him I was leaving with or without him. He ended up being ready on time and I drove. At the end of service during the call for Salvation, I walked up by myself, confessed the Lord as my Holy Savior, and joined the church! After service, he asked me why I went up there without him. He then criticized me for going up in front of the church by myself, and he told me that if I wanted to join, I should have just done it alone- after church. I couldn't believe it!

I started becoming convicted (and irritated) by our living situation. When we attempt to get our lives in order spiritually, we become convicted by things that we are doing that are out of order. I knew that living with a man that I was not married to was not right. I also knew that I was in a dead-end relationship with someone I would never choose to marry, and I was wasting my time hoping for a sunshine that he would never provide. I wanted my life to change, and I knew that I had to do something differently. I wanted to live right.

I dissolved our business, ended our relationship, and put him out of my house. Then I had the locks changed immediately. Shortly thereafter, I was once again blessed with full-time salaried employment.

I became serious about my spiritual journey with reading Proverbs and taking the time to pray. Then I learned about fasting and decided to participate in one. My pastor was promoting a fast called "Do 42" which involved 42 days of changing your diet along with certain behaviors. I wasn't quite ready to only eat steamed or raw vegetables, so I decided to partake in another related fast called "The 40 Day Fast". The 40 Day Fast did not involve completely abstaining from particular foods; instead, it requires one to focus on the Spirit for 40 days by doing things to avoid the 7 deadly sins: Lust, Sloth, Greed, Pride, Wrath, Envy, and Gluttony. The 40 Day Fast changed my life forever because it forced me to become more aware of every thought that crossed my mind, every word that I spoke, and every action that I made. It made me become more mindful and intentional in my living, and I encourage anyone who needs a spiritual jumpstart to dedicate 40 days of their life to transforming their spirit. If you are interested, you can find out more information about the fast at www.40day.com.

Reading the Bible, going to church, and fasting are not enough to implement real change, but it's a good starting point. I know and have seen people who can recite scripture and pray over you one moment, and act like Satan's child the next moment. What's important is having a relationship with the Creator, which is created by prayer, and actually living what you learn and know. We should all seek to have a relationship with God, not just religion. A person can go through the motions of what they consider to be practicing religion, but those motions are not enough to build a true and authentic relationship with God. Building a relationship takes patience, prayer, and productivity. We should be patient with ourselves in cultivating new habits. We should begin and end each day with prayer followed by a brief period of meditation, and we should be productive by allowing our actions to reflect what we are learning through our studying of the Word and revelations received through our prayer lives.

One thing that I did not want to be was a hypocrite. As a child, I saw hypocrites around me- folks who would attend church, pray, and act holy sanctified one moment, and were getting drunk, talking crazy, and acting unholy the next. I really began to live the Word for myself by trying to control my words about and towards others, developing a stronger attitude of giving, and overall making wiser decisions. It took me some time and I still made mistakes in between. But once I felt myself backsliding into my old ways, I got miserable of being miserable, continued to search out God for myself, and learned to be content and trust Him.

When I seriously got my relationship with God on track, I saw my life turn around before my eyes. I still encountered difficulties, but the difficulties that I faced were far easier to deal with than they were when I was on my own vice and relying on my own strength and "wisdom" to live life.

Short and sweet, when you truly put God first and allow your life to reflect that choice, you will find your life coming together, slowly, but surely.

"Love the Lord, your God, with all your heart, and He will give you the desires of your heart."– Psalms 34:4

Pearl

2

Become a Positive, Goal Oriented Person

The world is filled with so much negativity. From the time we wake up in the morning and turn on the television or radio, we are bombarded with news that drains our spirits and emotions.

Each day, stressors and negative information and influences constantly bombard us. It would do us great good to establish a positive mentality and spirit, and surround ourselves with others who are positive as well.

Positive people help to keep you motivated by sharing their optimism and enthusiasm. Positive people are more likely to express gratitude for what they have as opposed to complaining about what they don't have. They are also more likely to find a lesson to be learned or an opportunity for growth when in the midst of a difficult or uncomfortable situation, as opposed to allowing themselves to become mentally defeated when confronted with challenges.

Sometimes the people at my job can get in a habit of complaining about their pay, the work that they do, and many other things. I am even guilty of falling into this trap. Pessimism absolutely does not fix the problem. If anything, complaining makes you find other things to be negative about and then you attract other people who begin complaining about the things that they don't like, and the cycle continues. A solution is never reached-you just waste your time complaining and more than likely, you feel worse after the complaining session than you did when you first started talking about how you felt.

One thing that I have learned over the years is that we can change how we feel by changing our words, changing our thoughts, and being overall more positive. For instance, one morning I was driving to work, and this guy cut in front of me and almost hit my car. I was furious. Instead of letting it blow over, I did something really stupid...I let my window down. Needless to say after our exchange of words, I was even angrier. I continued to drive, furious, and mumbling all kinds of things under my breath. And then it hit me. I wasn't being positive, and I was allowing someone that I didn't even know to steal my joy. I had to counter the anger that I was feeling in order to get rid of the emotion, so I chose to change my feelings. I began speaking "I'm thankful that the man didn't hit my car", "I'm thankful for no traffic this morning", and "I'm thankful that I made it to work safely". I had to speak these words of gratitude so that I could hear them. Hearing them really made my anger subside and I was able to walk into work happy and ready to take on another day.

When you are positive, you will attract other positive individuals into your life. If you have a lot of drama in your life and in your relationships, you may want to check your own attitude and how you contribute to the problems that you face.

If you feel that your life is not headed in a fruitful direction, immediately evaluate yourself and analyze your circle such as the people that you hang around. Do you find yourself hanging around gossipers, pessimists, and complainers? People who are jealous of other folks' accomplishments, but who do not take full advantage of the opportunities with which they are presented? If so, you may want to seriously consider making some changes within yourself and within your circle so that you can attract more happiness and fulfillment into your life.

This brings me to another point: There were people, other female acquaintances that I thought that I wanted in my life. I have always been a loner type with a very small number of friends. Now, I know a million people, but as far as friends? Just real, true friends? I can count the number on one hand. Even if you are a positive person, you may not have a large circle of friends. But you have to pray and trust that God will send the right people who need to be in your life, at the right moment, for the right reason, and during the right season.

If you want to constantly improve in your life, make a commitment to thinking and acting in a more positive manner and work towards self-development to achieving your personal goals. When you do this, you will attract others to you with the same type of attitude. Not only will they serve as a support system, but they will also be your accountability partners by offering motivation, an encouraging word, and even constructive criticism in the event you begin to become lazy and stray away from accomplishing your personal and professional endeavors.

Pearl

Self-Educate and Read, Read, and Read Some More!

Studies show that a love for literature begin in the womb with the mother reading to the child or during the infancy/toddler stages when parents set aside a time in the afternoon or evening for reading. If you did not grow up loving to read, it is not too late!

I cannot begin to stress the importance of reading. Not only does reading oil your brain, keeping it moving, working, expanding, and growing, but reading consistently helps you become a better reader and writer. Reading also builds your vocabulary and language skills. It doesn't matter whether you are young or old, reading is an essential and invaluable skill to have.

You don't have to be enrolled in school or some type of educational program to read. Reading is a fundamental skill that everyone should have. If you are not confident in your reading abilities and you feel that you need to improve, check with your local library for reading classes. Public libraries oftentimes offer many classes for free. Continuing your education is not necessarily limited to going back to school to get a degree. If you read about how to improve your cooking by learning about proper food pairing, combining, and recipes, you are still continuing your education. When you read non-fiction, you are generally continuing your education by simply reading things to expand your knowledge base on a topic.

Sometimes you may prefer a good magazine, newspaper, tabloid, or adult novel, which can make for some great girl-talk, discussions, and debates. What matters is that you keep your brain and imagination alive. Expanding your mind and knowledge base will allow you to hold meaningful conversations with many different types of people. Also, reading different genres helps you to be more aware of the thoughts, feelings, opinions, and perspectives of others, which can help you identify with them. Being able to relate and connect to others is important for building your network.

The awesome thing about technology is that you can now download a book on your Kindle or other electronic device, or even listen to an audio-version of a book. Long gone are the days where you have to carry around bulky books. You can download and carry hundreds of books on one small electronic device and listen to it if you so please.

I would challenge you to read (or listen to) at minimum, two books per month. It is easy to make time. Give up one of your favorite shows and dedicate at least thirty minutes every night to reading something that you can learn from. If you don't have time to read, you can choose to listen to an audio book in your car, while walking, or while cleaning the house. Create or join a book club that reads books of a genre that interests you. If you are constantly learning, you are constantly growing. Reading allows you to become exposed to many different things that otherwise you many not know about. Learn as much as you can about everything that you can. No one can ever take away what you know.

Pearl

Exercise, Eat Right, Keep Your Body Tight

W hen you're young, your body is in its prime. You can eat whatever you want and whenever you want, usually without considering whether or not what you're eating is good for you.

What many people don't understand is that the habits that you have during your youth will appear when you get older. And by older, I don't mean in your sixties or seventies, I mean in your late twenties. There are so many people that I went to high school with, who, by the time we reached our ten year high school reunion, had gained so much weight and looked like completely different people. Social media allows us to stay in touch with people for decades and we can see the changes (good and bad) that people make over time.

Maybe you are one of those people (like my sister) who eat the worst foods and never gain weight. Although your poor food choices may not reflect on your outward appearance, they can definitely manifest as hidden maladies such as high cholesterol, blood pressure, or diabetes.

I'm a southern gal from the country. I was born in Columbus, Georgia. I grew up on chitterlings, barbecued ribs, rib tips (my grandmother made the best), smothered pork chops, fried chicken, ham hock, greens, buttermilk cornbread, macaroni and cheese,

cheese grits, pork bacon and biscuits, and Chester's BBQ- your typical southern foods that are known to contribute to high blood pressure, diabetes, and a host of other diseases.

I ate these foods and more growing up. The ice cream truck that came through the neighborhood sold chips, Faygo soda, and pickled pigs' feet. Every neighborhood had a Candy Lady who would sell all kinds of chips, candies, gums, sodas, and if you were lucky, popsicles. The old folks in the neighborhood would drink their Co-Cola with peanuts in it. Older folks in the family would chew and spit snuff. We lived a peaceful life, but a lot of these same people were overweight, on several medications, and suffered from illnesses such as hypertension, high cholesterol, and later on, different types of cancers. They could barely walk long distances or walk without a cane. As I became older, I realized that many of these diseases were directly related to poor diet and lack of exercise.

My diet during middle and high school consisted of more junk: candy, Burger King double cheese burgers, Flaming-Hot Cheetos, and any kind of junk food you can imagine. This was back when they sold the really tall bag of Hot Cheetos for only $1 and they were really, really hot. I ate an entire bag every single day after band practice. I ate a lot of calorie-packed foods that were devoid of nutrients and I hardly ever ate an appropriate amount of dark leafy greens and vegetables.

Despite my horrible diet, I never gained weight in high school because I was very active in the marching band. However, the effects of my diet reared itself in other areas. For example, I had the most agonizing menstrual cramps known to man. I remember having menstrual pain so bad that I couldn't even walk. I began to loath my period as it approached every month. I hated being a female just because of the unbearable pain that my period caused me every month. I lost sleep. Sometimes I would wake up in the middle of the night crying and get in the bed with my mother. I was good and seventeen, crawling in the bed with my mom. Midol, Excedrin, drinking extra water, nothing helped to ease the pain that I felt every month. I knew that I could not and did not want to live the rest of my life that way.

That was my beginning to health and wellness.

In 1999, my sophomore year in high school, I decided to go natural with my hair and stop eating pork. It was difficult to stop eating pork because everyone in my family ate it, so I merely decreased my intake. It wasn't until my freshman year in college when I was actually fully able to stop eating pork and beef. When I eliminated beef, pork, and sodas from my diet, I saw an immediate change in my menses. My cycle was now bearable and I didn't have the atrocious pains that I had in high school. It improved even more as I continued to exercise and improve my diet through becoming a vegetarian. By the end of my junior or senior year in college, I was able to have a menstrual cycle and not have to take any type of pain reliever. Along with my diet, the length and flow of my cycle changed as well. I went from a seven-day super heavy period, to a four-day cycle with only one and a half heavy days.

Eating balanced does so much more than improve our physical appearance. Proper diet and exercise increases our blood flow and improves the strength, health, and vitality of our inner organs. In addition to eating better, we must make sure that we exercise on a regular basis. 30 minutes of cardio at least 3 times a week will get your heart pumping and blood flowing. I firmly believe that women's diseases such as fibroids, endometriosis, uterine cancers and the like begin in our youth due to dietary choices and an influx of estrogen hormones via birth control. Had I not made the dietary changes that I made at a young age, I'm certain that I would be affected by some of these diseases today.

If you know that you need to make a change to live a healthier lifestyle make the change! There are so many health-food alternatives that were not popular a decade ago such as almond and rice milks, dairy-free cheeses, meat alternatives, gluten-free foods, different types of sweeteners, and information on it all by way of reading material, television, or the web.

It's better to take care of yourself now than to wait until your body breaks down and you are prescribed numerous medications to try to remedy the situation. Be proactive. Go for a walk around your neighborhood or at the nearby track at your school. After a while, upgrade your walks to running and walking intervals. If you go to the track to exercise, jog the straight lanes and walk the curves. Incorporate an app like "Couch to 5K", which uses running and walking intervals to help go from a couch potato to running five kilometers (3.1 miles). Incorporate calisthenics and simple exercises like sit-ups, crunches, pushups, tricep dips, squats, and lunges into your routine to get and keep your body tight and firm. Monitor the foods and drinks that you intake into your body. Eat something green with every meal.

Some changes that you can make to create a healthier life include:

- Drink at least half of your body weight in ounces of water each day. Dehydration is often the culprit behind bad skin, migraines, and a host of diseases and ailments. Dehydration has even been cited as being as cause of pre-term delivery in pregnant women.
- Limit or totally eliminate your consumption of sodas and sugary products.
- At lunch and dinner, make sure ¼ of your plate contains a green vegetable.
- If you are in a rush and you opt for fast food, substitute a side salad in place of fries.
- Try to incorporate a veggie day into your diet at least once a week i.e. "Meatless Mondays".

Choose healthy habits so that the bad habits don't end up choosing you.

Pearl

Become Financially Literate

G rowing up, I used to sit beside my grandmother while she balanced her checkbook and created a budget. I didn't know how she did it, but I used to observe her daily routine of adding, subtracting, and analyzing her finances. However, I didn't see my mother and father incorporate these same practices. This is not to say that they didn't; I just didn't see them do it. Regardless, my mother used to always tell us to save money but I never really understood why. I knew it was important to save, but I just didn't understand why we couldn't enjoy the money that we had. As a result, when I got ten or twenty dollars here and there, I usually spent it on candy, junk food, a calling card so that I could put minutes on my phone (this was before the unlimited cell phone plans) or purchase whatever other minute things that I desired.

By the time I entered high school and got my first job, my mother helped me to open up a bank account. However, I spent much of my money on clothes, shoes, jewelry, and electronics. I still didn't really understand the importance of saving.

Fast forward to my first year of college. Oh, how I wish that I had saved all of the monies that I earned while working double shifts at the movie theater my junior and senior years of high school. I had a work study job, barely any money, and I had to learn how to budget so that I could purchase essentials such as soap, toothpaste, washing powder, snacks, gas for my car, and my cell phone bill. It also seemed as if every time I walked into the student center, there was a company promoting their products and trying to get us to sign up for credit cards. Many students took the bait. I did not. The most that I knew about credit cards was that those who I knew who had them had a lot of debt, which was something that I didn't want. I was terrified of credit cards. Thus, I had no credit.

In all the reading, studying, and learning that I did in college, I never took the time to learn about finances and how to properly manage them. I didn't know the real purpose of a savings account or the different types of savings accounts available. I had no real knowledge about investments, stocks, bonds, and mutual funds. I didn't know or understand what credit was, the importance of it, how to establish it, and how to keep it in good standing.

Credit

Credit is something that one person or company provides to another person or company and the receiving company or individual is allowed to postpone reimbursement for a period of time. For instance, let's analyze a credit card. Credit card companies issue lines of credit to individuals for various amounts. An individual can charge (or purchase) goods until they reach the maximum amount that they were issued (for example, you receive a card with a $100 credit limit and you purchase $100 worth of items or services, although it is not recommended that you max a credit card out at any time).

When you purchase a credit card, you have free reign to buy as you please. But it comes at a cost. Many credit card companies charge a small percentage to maintain a balance on the card, which is known as interest.

Your credit score is pretty much a reflection of your payment history. So for that $100 that you charged on your Visa credit card, say you have until the 15th of every month to pay a minimum balance of $10. You pay the credit card bill every month until it is paid off. If you pay the minimum balance of $10/month, it will take you nearly a year to pay off the balance, plus you will incur interest fees. However, if you pay $50 a month, you can have the card paid off in two months and your credit score will reflect a good payment history.

Your credit score is updated almost every three to four months by three reporting agencies: Equifax, TransUnion, and Experian. It is recommended that you pull your credit report annually from each of the three credit bureaus to stay informed and also ensure that no identity theft has occurred.

One of my first introductions to credit cards came during my senior year in high school. My friend, Dee, started wearing really nice clothes and outfits to school every single day. She dressed nice beforehand, but now, she REALLY looked nice. I asked her about her upgrade and how she did it. She confided to me that she had went and purchased a department-store credit card and went shopping, but now she had to pay the money back. A few years later, when I was in college, I was told something similar by an acquaintance of mine. This young lady, Tiana, would purchase expensive pairs of jeans and pay for it by using a store credit card. I asked her how she managed the bill, since I knew she was a full time student and wasn't actively working. She told me that she just paid the minimum balance each month. Paying the minimum balance is fine if your only goal is to fulfill your payment obligations; however, it is not a wise course of action if your goal is to pay the balance off and become free of credit card debt.

My learning didn't stop there. During my senior year, my mother took it upon herself to order me a credit card so that I could establish my credit. I was upset with her initially, but I later realized that my anger came from being scared. I didn't want a credit card because I didn't want to get into debt. Before the card reached my hands, one of my family members, who knew that my mother ordered the card for me, asked if they could charge their car repair on my card. This family member had helped me out in college by helping me purchase books, so I said okay, and I took her word for it when she said that she would repay me. Long story short, $1500.00 was charged to my card and eventually, I ended up paying the amount back, plus interest, before the card was shut off by the company! I learned several lessons:

- It is better to establish credit using a credit card with a low limit
- Pay your credit card bills on time
- Do not lend your personal credit to anyone because you will be responsible for their debt

Following college, I got my first real job. I also purchased my dream car...a convertible BMW. My BMW was so sweet. It was jet black with chrome accents and brick red interior. I loved that car and received attention everywhere I went. But I didn't love the price of maintaining the car. No one told me about the price of purchase and maintenance of low profile tires, and how expensive basic maintenance (such as oil changes, alignments, having brakes replaced, having the tires rotated and balanced) on foreign cars can be. Prior to purchasing my BMW, I didn't realize the price difference between regular and premium gas. My car purchase was eating my pockets away.

Shortly after purchasing my car, I was able to purchase a home. I tried to stay modest with my home purchase, so I purchased a foreclosed townhome for a very reasonable price. Although my home was affordable, all of my debt and bills made life financially uncomfortable.

So many of us are so misinformed about finances that it's ridiculous. If it's one piece of advice that I can share with you to prevent you future heartache and stress, it's simply this: live beneath your means. Do not trap yourself into a sea of debt and become a slave to these predatory credit card companies by trying to look nice and wear certain types of clothes. You can shop on a budget and still look fantastic.

I had to take a second job to make ends meet and pay bills. I would teach all day, and immediately go to T-Mobile where I worked until 10 or 11 at night. I was exhausted. I lived to work and worked to pay bills. I had a brand new house that I wasn't able to enjoy because I was always working. Even still, the money that I had left over after paying bills, I used it to go shopping. I still had not learned my lesson.

It wasn't until my late twenties, after the birth of my daughter, that I stopped the negative financial cycle. I stopped spending frivolously and eating out all of the time. I started cooking more. I began reading Dave Ramsey's books to learn how to establish a budget and get out of debt. I released the need for immediate gratification, and settled for staying in to save money as opposed to going out to spend money. Within a year and a half's time, most of my bills were paid off and my credit score increased by over a hundred points.

Don't be like me and many other young people living for the now, spending money because you have it to spend. Create a plan. Imagine what you want your life to be one, three, five, and ten years from now financially. Write down steps you are going to do to accomplish your goals.

Unfortunately, there are older adults who still manage their money improperly. These people do not pay their bills on time because they spend money on other things. In some cases, they overspend and live above their means, purchasing things they cannot afford. Don't allow the problems of these people to affect you and how you manage your money, especially if it's friends and close family. I have learned that it's one thing to help someone, but it's another thing to enable their bad habits. Don't allow your friends and family to guilt you into helping them out because of their own poor management skills.

Another thing that I learned about a budget is that you can fit everything in it. You can set aside money for recreation, shopping, and even things such as purchasing gifts for special occasions, birthdays, and baby showers. The key is to stick to it and be consistent. Don't be afraid or ashamed to turn down a night on the town with your friends in order to save some money. Allow your goals and the desire to achieve your vision be your drive.

Don't be misled by the appearances of others. Many people with the nicest clothes and cars cannot always afford them. You would be surprised at the number of people who live in the biggest houses, driving the luxury cars, who are drowning in a sea of debt and living check to check. This not only includes friends, family, and random people that you see in society; this also applies to many popular celebrities, who rent many of the things that they floss in public as opposed to actually owning it.

Learn as much as you can about finances and budgeting. I recommend reading material by authors such as Dave Ramsey and Suze Orman. Additionally, the "Dummies" reading series offers several selections for financial novices that may help to establish a basic foundation of financial literacy and wisdom.

Here are some brief suggestions to remain financially healthy:

- Get a credit card with a low limit to establish good credit. Make sure that you make small charges and pay the balance off at the end of every month.
- Never co-sign anything for anyone, regardless of who they are.
- Don't allow people to use your credit card and trust them to pay you back. If you have the money to give, give cash without expectation of reimbursement. In rare instances would I help someone out in this manner, and it would only be because they have shown and proven that they can be trusted in regards to matters of money.
- Get a credit card with a low balance (not more than $500) to establish your credit. Never charge over half of the card. Double up on the payments and pay the card off as quickly

as you can. If you know that $500 is too much for you and you would be tempted to spend it, start out with a card that only has a $100 credit limit.

- Pay all of your bills on time.
- Shop clearance and sales items. Research the best deals on expensive goods.
- Each month, establish a zero-balanced budget and stick to it.
- When purchasing a car, take into consideration the gas mileage, costs of tag and monthly insurance, and price of gas and maintenance.
- Learn about retirement plans and different types of investments.

Pearl

Choose What *Is* Right
Instead of What *Feels* Right

There come times in life where we may meet someone who seems like the perfect match. His mere presence drives you crazy. He may be tall, charming, muscular, and have a beautiful smile with pearly white teeth. When you hug him, you can nestle your body up against his chest and lay your head there ever so gently. He wraps you in his arms and you feel warm and safe. You inhale his cologne, his scent, and his essence. Your connection and chemistry is amazing. The conversations flow easily. You both vibe together. You can feel his energy and his emotions and are overwhelmed with a feeling of euphoria. You think about him consistently; and he tells you he does the same. When you two are together, it's like you two are the only ones who exist in that moment and time. It feels good. It feels right.

Despite the amazing connection, something just isn't right. Maybe it's just a feeling that you can't quite put your finger on. Or maybe this Mr. Wonderful has shown some glimpses of being jealous, controlling, or possessive. You see how he curses and hits his dashboard in a fit of road rage or when he gets irritated. Maybe he has a habit of overspending and living above his means. Or he has an ex or a baby mama with whom the lines of obligation seem blurry and he is not the most forthcoming with information about the level of their relationship. Maybe the timing is just off and you two are in two different places in your lives. You may share intimate moments with him…a kiss, a hug, or you may express yourself sexually. Then, his routine changes. He stops answering your calls and he disappears for a period of time, only to resurface a few months later.

If there is one thing that I have learned in my experience, it's that God is not the author of confusion. If a person is meant to be in your life, there will be no inner apprehensions or hesitations in your gut. If a situation is meant for you, there will be no drama that accompanies it. You won't have to question this man's actions, inquire as to why he's no longer calling, wonder why he switched his routine, or conduct yourself as if you're "walking on eggshells" in order to avoid an unkind response or criticism from this person… regardless of how good it FEELS to be with this person. It feels good, but in the back of your mind and in your heart of hearts, you know that being with them is not the best decision for you.

The first definition of love given in the book of 1 Corinthians 13, verse 4 states "Love is patient and kind". Patience is the ability to live your life without harboring or constantly thinking or dwelling about a particular person or thing. Patience allows you to see who a person really is and what they are about. Time tells all and time reveals all by allowing you to analyze the person and getting to know them and the details of their character. It's quite possible that you may decide that you may be better off as friends, or that you really don't like them as much as you initially thought after all. If someone is for you, they will be there. They will be there one month or ten months down the road, and their actions will be consistent. There is no need to rush and jump into a relationship or hold on to someone that you know with your better judgment that you probably shouldn't be dealing with.

Infatuation and lust can interfere with the process of getting to know someone because they both create emotions that cloud our senses and judgment. Once intimacy (of any form) has been introduced, we tend to dwell on the euphoric feelings that occur as opposed to remain sensible and levelheaded about the person and the situation. As a result, we tend to accept behaviors and ignore traits that are red flags to warn us to slow down and take our time. In some cases, the red flags show us that we need to run far, far away.

Don't make the mistake of ignoring your intuition and red flags just because something feels right, when you know deep down inside that the person or situation is not right for you.

Oftentimes, that "gut feeling" that you feel in the pit of your stomach is God speaking to you to guide you. Follow it. Listen to it. Your intuition will never lead you wrong.

The Pearls of
Love & Relationships

Pearl

Protect Your Heart

Proverbs 4:23 states in the New International Version, "Above all else, guard you heart, for everything you do flows from it."

From my experience, us women can be way too trusting when it comes to our hearts. Many of us have been wrongly led to believe that we must compete with other women and prove our worth to a man up front in order to gain his affections and the number one spot on his priority list.

As a result, we put our best foot forward. We make him meals to demonstrate our cooking abilities, we dress our best at all times, making sure to look impeccable and smell delectable. Some of us may start posting pictures of him all over our social media accounts, and tagging him in every picture and status that we write about him. And in our minds, we start placing his last name onto our first name and thinking about the future: dating, meeting the family, and asking ourselves "Could this be the one?"

Emotionally, we go from 0 to 100 in no time and we become attached. We become attached not to him, but to the idea of him, the idea of him being the one, and the idea of him being the one who will love us and fully accept us, flaws and all.

If we make the decision to be sexually intimate with the gentleman, the intimacy can seal the deal even more for us as women, especially if the illicit sex is pleasing. Oftentimes, we become more emotionally bonded to a man after having sex repeatedly. And what happens next? We fall in love with someone, who more often than not, we barely know and we allow them the keys to our heart. We become mentally and emotionally married to a man who has not even considered proposing to us.

Ladies, protect your heart. Don't treat a boyfriend like a husband. Boyfriends come and go. Regardless of the lifestyle that modern culture promotes, don't be too quick to sleep with a man. If a man really likes you, he will date you without having sex. Don't withhold sex just to try to get him to "prove himself". Practice abstinence for yourself and be clear on why you are doing it. Your reasoning could be to honor God or to honor yourself. Many women get attached and grow strong feelings for someone once they decide to be sexually intimate. The feeling of having sex without knowing whether or not the relationship will "work out" or even be going strong six months later can be disconcerting. Practicing abstinence helped me to have a peace of mind and peace in my spirit when it came to relationships. Being abstinent helped me to remain focused on myself and my purpose, and it helped me to see beyond the "representative"— the image of a person that is presented to you when you are getting to know someone. Remaining abstinent helped me to pay more attention to the conversations and thoughts of a suitor as well as scrutinize their actions and intentions. It helped me to get rid of the weeds that were trying to sprout in my new-found garden of life.

Protecting your heart does not only apply to lovers. This pearl can also apply to family members and so-called friends. We may have family or friends who may have abandoned us, or who may have just done some down-right low down, dirty things to us. They may envy us, or they may feel that we wronged them in some capacity, and instead of communicating their grievances, they may hold a grudge. Even if they choose to communicate they may still hold a grudge after we apologize. One thing that I had to learn the hard way was that we all have our separate paths in life. We all make our own choices. Just because someone is blood-related does not mean that you have to take on their issues as your own. It also doesn't mean that you have to subject yourself to someone's disrespect and mistreatment.

You can guard your heart by doing three things:

1. Choose who you love and the way that you love wisely
2. Love toxic relatives from a distance. Be nice and cordial but don't allow yourself to get upset when your expectations aren't met.
3. Cut relationships with toxic friends and be open to meeting new friends.

More than anything, guard your heart. When we are emotionally distressed, sadness and depression can affect all areas of our lives. Many people overeat and engage in destructive behavior (excessive drinking, drug use) when they are sad and feeling down. As a result, they may gain a lot of weight or establish bad habits that can adversely affect your health, wealth, and quality of life. On the flip side, when people live a life of happiness and joy, they tend to have a glow about them and their mere presence can brighten up a room.

Guard your heart and choose whom you allow to enter its four chambers wisely.

Pearl

Don't Choose a Mate Based on Potential

What is potential? Dictionary.com defines potential as "possible as opposed to actual".

I used to be that girl who could see into people and liked what I thought they could be: "Oh, he's an artist. He's very talented and has a great gift. His artwork has been featured on various prime time television shows and he paints live every week at a popular Open Mic."

Or "He's sooooo fine. He's tall, muscular, has a great sense of humor, and is a popular fraternity with great connections. He's a brilliant entrepreneur and is also pursuing a Master's Degree."

Or "He's has his own studio and production company. He travels and performs at various venues and cities. He's from up North and has that New York swagger. His voice sounds amaaazing."

It is often easy for us to recognize the positive qualities and attributes of a person while ignoring the obvious: he is handsome and charming (but he has several children by different women and does not fulfill his responsibilities as a father), he is successful and educated (but he is unfaithful and he is a liar), he is articulate with a degree from Morehouse (but he also is a convicted felon who still partakes in illegal activities), he attends church on a regular basis, takes care of his children and loves the Lord (but he is physically and emotionally abusive).

A very long time ago, my brother told me that you can't look at someone for their potential and who you think they will become; you have to look at them for where they are at the time because some people may never change. I have to say that his statement stuck with me and I think that there's a lot of truth to it.

Sometimes we can see different personality characteristics within someone and we know that if they channel their focus and energy in the proper way, those characteristics can help propel them forward and may attribute to their success. However, it is important to remember that just because we recognize good things in others doesn't mean that they recognize those same characteristics within themselves; and even more so, it doesn't mean that they want to develop and use those traits.

Instead of focusing on someone's stagnant energy and potential, focus on what exactly they show you when you are with them. If they are making real, true strides to improving their life and their character, then they may be worth keeping around. However, if all they are giving you is pipe dreams to believe in and not really supporting their statements with their actions, then you may want to consider removing them from your life because such connections can be toxic especially when the connection is that of a romantic nature.

There is no quicker way to lose focus and be distracted from your path than to get involved with a man whose path and plan is distorted and unclear.

Pearl

Learn to Love Yourself before You Try to Love Someone Else

I once met a woman who was a beautiful, smart, and intelligent. She commanded attention when she graced a room with her presence. She was thoughtful and could be outspoken on social and cultural issues. She was articulate. She could also create amazing, colorful pieces of clothing, home décor, and jewelry with her hands. She was creative. Her style was urban afro chic. She didn't give into the popular trends and fads, however, she was stylish in her own right and she wore her clothing with confidence. Women her age saw her and envied her, thinking that she had her life all together. She graduated from college in three and a half years, Summa Cum Laude, without ever having to pay a dime. She matriculated throughout college on an academic scholarship and her education was paid for. Before she graduated, she had plenty of job offers because she was great at what she did. When she chose to change her location, she picked up another job without a problem. After a brief stint living with her parents, she eventually purchased her dream car, a convertible luxury BMW and her own house. She even started her own business.

Beneath the entire exterior, this woman was sad and depressed. She really didn't have any standards on who she chose to allow into her life, and worse, she didn't really know how to set standards without seeming materialistic. She had been a victim of the "Falling for Potential" guys, who ended up hurting her emotionally. She was looking for love in all the wrong places. She was looking for love in the faces of different people instead of looking inside and looking towards God. I knew this woman very well. This woman was me.

It's simple. I got myself into some bad situations because I didn't love myself, and I honestly didn't know how. I mean, did I care about myself? Sure! I made sure that I looked nice, kept myself up, and had money in the bank. But I didn't really understand what genuinely loving myself looked like, or what it really meant. Thus, I was completely incapable of truly loving someone because I simply didn't know how to.

The Law of Attraction is very real when it comes to relationships. Oftentimes, you attract what you are. I couldn't understand… I was a sweet person with a sweet spirit but I attracted some of what I thought were the ugliest people to me. In retrospect, these people were actually decent people; they just had some serious character flaws. After deep analysis, I began to realize that I often attracted the same spirit to me, just in the form of a different physical body; and these people were physical reflections of spiritual and emotional character and flaws.

At some point when you get tired of being tired, you must realize that YOU are the common denominator in all of your relationships-gone-wrong. If you want to see change, then you must change. If you want love, then you must give love. If you want respect, then you must give respect to yourself first before you give it to others.

What Loving Yourself Looks Like:

1. You consistently engage in activities that help to construct you and not destruct you
2. You take responsibility for your actions and you do not develop a "victim" mentality and attitude
3. You set standards and boundaries for yourself

4. You set standards and boundaries for people who you allow into your life.
5. You do not allow people to mistreat you or disrespect you
6. You refuse to accept abuse in any form: emotionally, mentally, physically, and verbally
7. You actively cultivate your spirit and character

1Corinthians Ch. 13 tells us what love is: "Love is patient, love is kind. It does not envy, it does not boast, it is not proud. It does not dishonor others, it is not self-seeking, it is not easily angered, it keeps no record of wrongs. Love does not delight in evil but rejoices with the truth. It always protects, always trusts, always hopes, always perseveres."

This verse does not just apply to loving others, but also to loving ourselves. You must be patient and kind to yourself. Don't boast about yourself or have a proud spirit, but have a spirit of humbleness. Don't dishonor others, and don't dishonor yourself. Don't keep a record of wrongs, staying upset with yourself for mistakes that you made in your past. Forgive yourself and move on. Protect yourself, trust your intuition, hope for the best, and keep pressing forward regardless of the circumstances.

Love yourself first- only then can you properly learn how to love others.

Pearl

Wrap It Up

L et me just begin this chapter bluntly. If you choose not to remain abstinent and you are not married, you need to use condoms any time you have sex. Every. Single. Time.

The use of condoms greatly decreases the chances of unplanned pregnancy as well as the contraction and spread of sexually transmitted diseases. Plain and simple. Even if you have been with a person for several months or several years, if you have not made vows and secured one another financially, there is no reason to have unprotected sex. Some people feel that when they are in a relationship with someone for a long time, then sex is okay.

Ladies, let me tell you, it is not a smart move.

Despite pop culture's obsession with sex, many monotheistic religions teach against fornication and stress the importance of waiting until marriage to have sex. Although abstinence can be a challenging concept to mentally grasp and daunting to physically practice, it is actually a method to keep you safe from deepened heartache, single parenthood, and sexually transmitted diseases. Now, although these things can occur otherwise, the chances are greatly decreased within a marriage and obsolete within the practice of abstinence.

Many people use what's referred to as the "pull-out method" to prevent pregnancy, which is where a couple engages in unprotected sex and the man removes his penis from the woman's vagina prior to ejaculation to prevent pregnancy. The pull-out method is not a 100% foolproof method of preventing pregnancy and sexually transmitted diseases. If you choose to have sex with someone who is not your husband, you need to use protection.

Some single women even go so far as to engage in family planning with boyfriends. Again, ladies, not a smart move. A man should want to formally commit to you in marriage before you "plan" to have children. Ladies, we have to be smart. We need to stop treating boyfriends like they are husbands. We cannot continue to put ourselves and our children in compromising situations because it "feels" good at the time. We cannot continue to give up the cookie, then complain when men don't accept all of their responsibilities because chances are, he showed you exactly what he was about from the very beginning. All of our moves and decisions must be calculating decisions. That doesn't mean that you need to be conniving; however, it means that prior to making decisions, you must think deeply about the various consequences and repercussions of your choices. Thoughtfulness can prevent you from putting yourself in a bad situation down the road.

I can't tell you the countless number of times that I've seen situations where a young lady had been dating someone for some time and he made her feel comfortable…making plans with her and telling her things that had her looking forward to the future. Since she was in love, of course she believed him. He told her he loved her and he wanted her to be the mother of his child and have his baby. She believed him. He told her that he would take care of her and the baby. She believed him. She got pregnant. Shortly afterwards, he left. All alone with a baby to care for, she became angry at his apparent lies, the rejection, and the abandonment. Even worse was the fear of having to raise a little one on her own. Sometimes, the women even choose to abort the child- living with the memory of that decision the rest of their entire life.

These are painful, preventable situations that many women find themselves in. Don't get me wrong, children are a blessing to have.

But the truth is, it is far easier to raise a child with two incomes and two parents contributing as opposed to one. However, if we make wiser decisions in the beginning, we may be able to avoid the pain and heartache that may ensue.

Diseases are running rampant in this country with youth and young adults accounting for a large percentage of new infections. I teach at a middle school and one of my sixth grade students confided to me that she recently lost her virginity. During our conversation, I informed her about the prevalence of sexually transmitted diseases that you could contract despite the use of condoms. She was extremely surprised, as the information that I shared with her was new to her. It is fairly easy for a woman to become infected with STD's such as syphilis, genital herpes, and Human Papilloma Virus (HPV) just by skin to skin contact. Yes, you can get one of these diseases even if you use condoms because condoms do not cover the entire genital area.

Now, if you still decide to engage in unprotected sex with your companion, I strongly urge you both to take a full physical and full STD blood screening and share the results with one another. Don't take the person's word for their results. Some people, regardless of how genuine they may seem, will lie to your face and will be dishonest by withholding information that you don't ask them about. Exchange STD results and talk about it. Get tested on a regular basis, at least twice a year, if you are in a sexual, monogamous relationship to someone with whom you are not married and once a year if you are married. Regardless of your marital status, you should always be well informed about your health.

If you have several sexual partners, you should get tested at least every three months, even if you use condoms. There are many clinics that offer free, 30 minute HIV swab tests. You can ask your local doctor or search online for free HIV screening clinics in your area.

It is important to remember that sex is much more of a spiritual act than it is a physical act. Yes, it feels good…but sex is more so an activity that bonds two people together. As the Bible says "the two become one flesh." Marriage is a representation of two becoming one after the exchange of vows, rings, and names. Sex is a physical act and the birth of a child is the physical manifestation of "two becoming one". They are all interconnected.

That means that you "become one" with anyone who you engage in sexual activity with and they leave a spiritual imprint on you... or create what's called a "soul tie". Did you ever wonder why it was so difficult for you to get over someone that you loved? You haven't seen or spoken to them, and you just can't shake them? It's because you are actually tied to them spiritually. Old soul ties can be broken through prayer and fasting. However, it's much easier if we refrain from making that connection to someone we're not married to in the first place.

After a merry-go-round and cycle of start-great-end-horrible relationships, I decided that something had to change. If you want something different, you have to do something different. That something different was me. I had to change. I decided to do the challenge in *A Knight in Shining Armor* by P.B. Wilson. The challenge requires you to devote a period of six months to God, focusing on Him and bettering yourself. For me, the change was gradual, but it ended with me being abstinent for a period of six months. Instead of six months, I chose to do the challenge for the remainder of 2014, which was a total nine months. Not only did the challenge require me to be abstinent, but I also could not entertain men in a romantic nature. This means that I did not give out my number, go on dates, or have boyfriends.

At the beginning of the seclusion, I wondered what I had gotten myself into, especially after I met someone who seemed like the perfect match. I felt like God was testing me. I kept praying about the situation and I knew that if I continued to entertain this man, then that would mean that I was putting my desire to be with him before my desire to honor my commitment of abstinence and no dating that I had made with myself and God. Hadn't that been the problem in all of my relationships that ended horribly? Didn't I put my desire to be in a relationship before honoring God as a Christian woman?

Didn't I put the needs of men ahead of my own needs, only to get hurt in the end? I had to stick to it. I told this man that God was not the author of confusion and that we needed to wait. In response this man also told me that he was not willing to wait to date me.

What a blow! But what a blessing! Sometimes what may seem like a disappointment may be God setting you up for something better than you could have ever imagined. Remember that!

I continued to remain focused on my sabbatical. When the loneliness set in, it became even harder to stay focused, but I did.

I learned several things during my period of abstinence:

1. Abstinence helps you to break bad habits that you created.
2. Abstinence helps you to get in tune with yourself, who you are, and what you like
3. A period of abstinence can help you to identify the traits in a mate that you are willing to deal with, and traits that are deal breakers.
4. Abstinence helps you to see behind the words of suitors-helping you to identify the true intentions of people.
5. Someone who is in love with you and really wants to be with you will do whatever it takes to be with you.
6. Someone who is in love with you will move heaven and earth to add happiness to your life.
7. The best way for women to keep from getting their hearts broken and ending up as single mothers is to keep their legs closed.

Following my period of abstinence, one of my male friends expressed interest in dating me. He actually expressed interest in dating me prior to my sabbatical but I would not entertain his advances due to my desire to successfully complete my "dating break", and he was supportive of my endeavors. He told me that he would be there at the end of my sabbatical—and he was. We dated, and two months later he proposed with a beautiful solitaire diamond ring in front of our family and friends. With the blessing of our parents, we married six days later at the Justice of the Peace.

Had I not honored God and dated the guy that I *thought* I liked instead of completing my sabbatical, I would have blocked God's blessing of matrimony to my life partner.

If you find yourself repeatedly trapped in a cycle of bad relationships, the best thing that you can do is remove yourself from the cycle and take a focused break from romantic relationships and sex.

You are the common denominator in your relationships. If you want change, begin with changing you.

Pearl

Always Follow Your Gut

"Following your gut" is a cliché that is oftentimes overused. So many people say it but fail to do it. What exactly does it mean, anyway? Does it mean to eat whatever food you a craving, whenever you crave it? Does it mean to cave in to the desires of your flesh? On the contrary. It means to do what's right for you and in your best interests, even if your emotions, heart, or flesh tells you otherwise.

Your gut feeling, otherwise known as your intuition, comes from a place deep inside of you. Some refer to that deep place as the soul, or the solar plexus. I'd like to think of it as God's way of speaking to you. When we are in tune with ourselves, we are able to hear the voice of intuition or sense the direction of it more strongly. When we have taken the time to build and foster a relationship with the Creator, be it by reading, praying, and meditating, that voice becomes a lot more clear and will oftentimes guide us as on what direction to take and what decisions to make.

Personally, one way my intuition was strengthened was through becoming serious about my prayer life and being intentional in regards to my actions and thoughts. I made it a habit to wake up at least thirty minutes earlier to incorporate daily Bible reading and prayer into my life. When I took up running as a way of staying fit, I would wake up and run with a group of women from 5:00a.m. to

6:00a.m. at least three times per week. On these days, I would listen to scripture via my audio Bible for about fifteen minutes, and then I would spend the remainder of my run praying silently. I strongly urge you create time daily for spiritual communion with the Creator.

It has been through prayer that my intuition strengthened. Eventually, it got to the point where God would literally send me signs. For example, I would have dreams revealing people and situations to me. One prayer that I would make a habit of praying was "God, if this person is not for me, please reveal their character and remove them from my life." It didn't fail that many times, my answer came within three days of me saying that prayer. For example, in one particular relationship, I had a really bad feeling but I didn't know why. No matter what, the feeling just would not go away. I prayed to God that He would show me in the physical what I was sensing in the spirit. Three days later, I got into an argument with my lover and his response was physical abuse. When I threatened to leave, my lover became angrier and even more aggressive. Talk about a sign from God! Unfortunately, in my mind I made an excuse for his actions and remained in the relationship for some time, much to my detriment.

There are no coincidences. Follow your intuition and pay attention to the signs that God shows you and the direction that you are pointed in. I would strongly advise you not to ignore this feeling or "knowing" that you may experience. Every single time that I have ignored the advice coming from my deepest, clearest, self, I have lived to regret not following what my gut was leading me to do.

Pearl

Embrace Being Single

Plainly put, so many women fear being alone. You can take the most beautiful girl in the world, and at some point in her life, usually following a break-up or after being single for a certain amount of time, she will get tired of being single. At one point and time in my life, I was this girl.

Prior to marriage, my longest relationship lasted for three years. It was not a happy three years, either. I really should have ended the relationship after a year, but I figured that I had already invested a year and I did not want that year to be wasted. I thought that maybe the relationship would improve. Needless to say that one wasted year evolved into three wasted years with the emotions to match. I could only blame myself for the wasted time because I was the one who controlled my decisions.

After the demise of my relationship with this guy, I had to recreate my identity. Being 21, book smart, and highly attractive, I lacked common sense from being too wrapped up and absorbed in someone else's world for too long. I had a lot of extra time on my hands. I was not focused and my spiritual life was no longer on track. I had become someone that I didn't know.

I didn't take the time to detox and learn myself again. I began to date around to try to ease the void and neutralize the feeling of being alone. I had plenty of friends. But for some reason, I felt alone. As a child who grew up in a house complete with mom and dad, brothers and sisters, aunts, uncles, and cousins (yes, we all lived together for years), I simply was not used to being alone. So I sought out places to go to and people to hangout with. However, these people and places didn't fill the void. I was still alone, and felt like I needed to be in a relationship.

How many of you have or have known people that have ping-ponged from relationship-to-relationship with hopes of finding your "soul mate" only to find someone that drains the energy from your soul? Have you ever settled for less than what you know you deserve because you don't want to be alone?

Don't be that girl who gets impatient with waiting to meet "Mr. Right" that you settle for "Mr. Right Now". Embrace your time being single.

Although single-hood can be looked down upon, it is an awesome time to develop an extremely strong relationship with the most important person in your life: you. Yes, you should be the most important person in your life, because if you don't take care of you, you won't be able to care for anyone else effectively.

When you are single, you don't have the distraction of trying to please someone else, maintain a relationship, or have someone consume your time. So take advantage of it!

Some things you can do during your single life include:

- Maintain your social life. Just because you are "alone" does not necessarily equate to loneliness. Go out with your friends, spend time with your family, and enjoy life!
- Invest your time in taking up a new hobby or learning a new skill. During some of my "single" moments, I did everything from taking sewing lessons, yoga classes, and to belly dancing lessons. I also began roller skating a lot and it helped to expand my network of friends. After the birth of my daughter and simultaneous divorce from her father, I took up running.

Not only did running help me to get in shape and lose the baby weight, but it was also a stress reliever and helped me release a lot of negative emotions that I was holding as a result of my divorce. Additionally, I met some great women and athletes through the "Black Girls Run!" organization, with whom I am still friends with today.

- Take time to read more books and expand your knowledge base. Read books on any and everything. You have a lot of extra time, so exercise your brain!
- Start a business. There are lots of ways to create a business. If you are good with computers, then create websites for people. If you are crafty, then sell items on Etsy, EBay, or Ravelry. Write a book. Make candles, body butters, and bath salts, and sell them. The options are limitless!
- Volunteer or become a mentor. Lend your services to those who need them most.
- Go back to school and expand your education and/or career
- Focus on becoming a better you. Work out. Exercise. Grow spiritually. Learn how to eat right. Get in the best shape of your life, on the inside as well as the outside.

There's so much to life to focus on than being in a relationship. As you focus on creating a better you, you will attract a better type of person to you. As you become more in tune with learning who you are, developing and establishing standards for yourself, you will be better prepared when another suitor enters your life. Hopefully you will be able to see any red flags that may arise, heed those warnings, and not waste your time.

Use your alone time as time to become more in tune with you. Before you expect to be treated good by someone else, you must first be good to yourself. Learn you, know you, and love you. Make sure that your spirit is one of forgiveness and is clear of emotional baggage. Only when you are whole will you attract a mate who is whole within themselves as well.

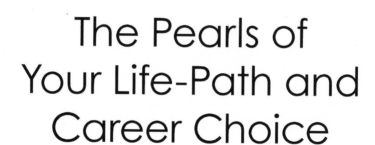

The Pearls of
Your Life-Path and
Career Choice

Pearl

Write the Vision and Make It Plain

It was 2006 when I was first introduced to the concept of creating Vision Boards. I was reading a book that was popular in New Age circles entitled *"The Secret"* by Rhonda Byrne. *"The Secret"* was a compilation of stories and advice from many successful persons; most of whom had overcome various obstacles and challenges in life to become huge successes. All of the featured persons had created a habit of speaking positively over their situations, thinking positively about circumstances which appeared bleak, visualizing their goals on a regular occurrence, and placing their goals in front of them in the form of physical representations called "Vision Boards".

Nowadays, so many people have heard of Vision Boards and at some point even participated in creating one. I created my first Vision Board in 2006 with a group of friends. We each brought scissors, a poster board, markers, at least 3 magazines, and a glue stick (we also brought food and wine and made it a girl's night).

I remember the first Vision Board that I created almost 10 years ago. I hung it on my wall, but over time, I didn't see myself moving closer to accomplishing anything I placed on that board.

As I experienced a series of relationships and trials in my personal life, I realized that my life and finances were moving further and further away from what was on my board. Then one day, I took it down and had to re-assess myself. What kind of person was I? Where was I emotionally, mentally, and spiritually? It seemed as if my spiritually-devoid life was crumbling all around me, until I was literally forced to give everything to God.

It was during that time that I realized that a plan without the grace of God is just that...a plan. Just because you created that plan for your life doesn't mean that that's what God wants for your life. And if your plan is not in your best interest or not in alignment with your Divine purpose, then the Universe will align things to occur that will constantly block you. Just because you created a Vision Board as a physical visualization of things that you want, doesn't mean that's what's in your best interest to have in the manner that you think you want it.

The Bible speaks of Vision Boards long before they were coined with that term. Habbakuk 2:2 states "Write the vision and make it plain, so that he may run who reads it". So often that quote is stated, and oftentimes people fail to realize what the following verse states: "For the revelation awaits an appointed time..." which means that everything has a pre-ordained timing with which it is to occur. Please understand that God's delay is not God's denial, and sometimes His "no" is a way of blocking us from harmful things that we may not be aware of at the time.

First, you need to be in alignment with yourself and with the Creator. You need to be clear and make sure that your goals line up with your passions and talents and not against them.

Secondly, before you begin constructing your Vision Board, pray on these things and that your desires be guided by God's heart and hand.

You may stare at that Vision Board and have faith that you hit the lottery for 4 million, or that you may get your dream job next month. However, even though you take the time to visualize your goals, remember that faith without works is dead. Success occurs when preparation meets with opportunity. Be mindful that even though we have created a wonderful picture collage that we would stare at and wish upon, the dream is all in vain until an appointed time. There is a time and a place for everything under the sun, so just because you glue a picture on a poster board and place it on the wall, doesn't mean that it will happen tomorrow. Oftentimes, visions take time and hard work to come to fruition.

So set your goals, pray about them, and pray over them. Write your vision, make it plain, and put them before you. Be patient, work diligently, and embrace the process. Learn to accept the good with the bad while you're on your journey to fulfilling your goals and dreams. Commit all your works to the Lord, and He will see you through.

Pearl

Discover Your Purpose

Imagine yourself lounging around your home on a rainy, lazy Sunday afternoon. You're bored. You call five of your friends and no one answers the phone. You turn on the television and out of 1,000 stations, nothing is on that you desire to watch. You're not tired and you don't exactly feel like cleaning any more. You begin thinking about tomorrow and the remainder of the week and a bit of dread overcomes you. You don't want to go to school or work. You know deep down inside of you that there has to be more to life other than waking up to go to school or work for someone else all day, just to come home and cook, eat, watch television, go to sleep, wake up and do the same thing all over again. You can feel it deep down inside of you that life has to offer more than just the mundane routine of going to school so you can work and live to pay bills for the rest of your life. What is your purpose? What are you put on Earth to do?

I am a sole believer that God created us all for a specific purpose, a specific thing to do and accomplish while we are here on Earth. Oftentimes, your purpose is in direct alignment with your talents, interests, and passions, and it doesn't have to necessarily be all that "deep". What I mean, for example, is that President Obama's purpose in life was to be who he is...to set history and become the first African-American President. Looking at his life story, it seems that from the beginning, his life groomed him towards his destiny. He is able to relate to many people since he is from a bi-racial background. He is able to relate to fatherless children. He graduated high school to study Law at Harvard University. And the story continues. His interests became his focus, which ultimately led him to his destiny.

I have met people who intentionally keep themselves busy doing a million and one things, thinking they are being productive. As a matter of fact, I used to be one of these people. These are people who wake up and are busy from the crack of dawn until they go to sleep because they find things to do. Whether it's going to work, going to school, and then volunteering on five different committees at church or in a social organization, by the time they get home, they are still lonely, bored, and feeling lost with a feeling of emptiness. Busyness does not mean that you are operating or working towards your purpose. Everything that you do should be purposeful and working towards a specific goal.

My advice to you is to analyze yourself. Ask yourself these questions:

- What things are you good at doing?
- What types of things do you enjoy?
- What brings you happiness and a sense of fulfillment?

If you can't answer these questions, it is time for you to cut off "Keeping Up with the Kardashians," stop wasting your time trying to emulate "The Real Housewives of Atlanta," and quit hoping for companionship while viewing "Love and Hip Hop." Use your time wisely and put your talents into practice. Learn a new skill or develop skills you already have. Use your talents to help others or produce something to bring other people joy. Seek God in faith and prayer for direction, and act on that direction through dedicating at least an hour a day towards studying or working on what you say you are passionate about.

We are all here to accomplish more than to simply participate in the routine of life. You were put here to do more than work, come home, watch television, and go to sleep-- just to wake up and do it all over again. Live with purpose and meaning and be intentional in your decisions and actions. Pray that God blesses the work of your hands as you allow your talents to fuel your passion and drive you towards fulfilling your purpose in life.

Pearl

Smoothing the Transition into Adulthood

There have been moments in life where I was in a state of "what do I do now?" My life was in front of me and I had no idea what to expect. Although I had a plan laid out, I had yet to act on that plan and there still remained feelings of fear coupled with uncertainty. I was in a place of the unknown.

Many young adults that I have known have experienced these same or similar emotions during major periods of transition. When you are faced with a major change, there is bound to be some sort of anxiety, especially if our plans go awry.

Each stage and time of transition is nothing more than a challenge, and it is this challenge which remains consistent throughout life. It's the same anxiety that's there when you matriculate from elementary to middle school, from middle school to high school, from high school to your profession, going from living a single life to being married, to having your first child, or to changing jobs. Each stage requires you to focus and redefine yourself and who you are. Each level requires a different level of effort and responsibility.

If angst sets in, just remember that change is the only thing that is constant in life. Embrace the changes and move forward with a positive attitude. Where possible, plan your work and work your plan. Plan your steps and your life. Where do you want to be in one year, three years, and five years? What steps are you going to take to work your plan and accomplish your goals?

As a teacher, I learned about the importance of creating S.M.A.R.T. goals for use in my classroom, and I feel that S.M.A.R.T. goals are useful in our personal lives as well. "S.M.A.R.T." is an acronym that stands for Specific, Measurable, Attainable, Realistic, and Timely. For instance, instead of setting a goal to state "I want to lose weight," a S.M.A.R.T. goal would state, "I will lose a total of fifteen pounds (Specific and Measurable) by exercising for one hour five days a week and eliminating sugar and fried foods from my diet (Attainable and Realistic) in three months (Timely)".

Write down your S.M.A.R.T goals. Keep them in a notebook and revisit them often to help you stay focused and on your path. If necessary, revise your plan. Accept change as a part of life and embrace it along with the many experiences and lessons that it brings.

Welcome the different levels of responsibility and put forward the required amounts of effort. Transitioning from a young lady to a responsible woman is a journey that is filled with twists and turns, mountains and valleys, but it is nothing to fear. Remain positive, focused, work hard and know that the best is yet to come.

Pearl

Avoid Assumptions
When Making Plans

A lot of young girls and women have a bad habit of planning life decisions around a male or love interest. This is a habit that oftentimes begins in high school during the dating process-- cancelling plans with your friends or family to spend time with someone, or even planning your college based on your love interest. For instance, there was a young lady named Simone who wanted to attend the University of Georgia in Augusta badly. However, Simone's boyfriend had decided to attend Albany State University located in Albany, GA. Simone did not want to be away from him, so she chose to attend Fort Valley State University (which was closer to Albany) instead of going to the University of Georgia in Augusta.

Needless to say, right before Simone had to report to FVSU for Freshman Orientation, her boyfriend broke up with her. She was devastated, not only because the boyfriend who she had strong feelings for had ended their relationship, but more so because she realized that she had sacrificed her personal desires for a young man who wasn't doing the same.

And there she was, stuck at a college that she didn't really want to attend just from trying to make a relationship work. Her decision was based on the assumption that she and her boyfriend would "work out." When they didn't, she had to deal the consequences of her decision. I've seen plenty of women do these types of things or place themselves in similar situations- relocate their jobs and their whole entire life to chase a boyfriend- girlfriend, only to arrive and be extremely unhappy.

I cannot say this enough. Do not make assumptions about anyone or anything when you make your plans.

Above all, do not create your plans around other people or what you think they will do. When you become married, then you will be required to make compromises along with your husband. Until that time arrives, do not make the mistake of giving boyfriends the same type of privileges and consideration that should be reserved for a husband. More often than not, most men will not give you the same type of consideration that you give him especially if their hearts and emotions are not truly invested in the relationship.

Men are going to do exactly what they want to do regardless of how you feel about it, so don't make sacrifices or decide not to pursue your personal desires based on someone else, because in the end, when the consideration is not reciprocated and you are left in the cold, you will have no one but yourself to blame. As a result, you will be forced to deal with the consequences of your decision in whatever form they may come.

Stay focused on your work, plan your work, and work your plan based on the goals that you want to accomplish as opposed to your assumptions about what you think someone else is doing or feeling.

The Pearls of
Being Social

Pearl

Maintain Your Connection with Your Circle

This chapter is dedicated to my best friend Chasity because she is the one who helped me realize how to keep friends, or better yet, maintain connections. I can be a very introverted person at times. Sometimes, I can get so wrapped up in things going on in my life, and when I want some company, I'm lonely. The two people closest to me (my husband and best friend Chasity) have a very active social life, know plenty of people, and talk to plenty of people on a regular basis. However, my life seems to revolve around work, my spouse and kids, taking care of home, and accomplishing my next task or goal.

You should never look on Instagram and compare your life to the lives of others (because other people's lives always look more exciting on the computer). But one day I did. One day after perusing Facebook and seeing some pictures of old college classmates still hanging out a decade after graduating, I asked Chasity how she thought they all managed to remain friends for so long. I asked her how she manages it also, since she has such a large social circle that she's been friends with for many years. Her answer was simple:

Find a way to keep in contact.

Whether it's a text where you reach out and see how they are, or an occasional call from time to time, maintain your connection with your friends by reaching out to link with them. Check on them, ask them questions, and inquire how they and their family are maintaining.

Sometimes, the people you surround yourself with may change over time, and that's natural. As we change and evolve, so should our circle. However, there are some people in life with whom we become good friends and have the possibility of transitioning into lifelong friends, but we have to put the work and effort into developing and maintaining our relationships.

Always create time to reach out to them to connect by doing the following:

- Call and/or text to check in occasionally
- Follow them on social media and interact with them
- Support and attend important events in their lives
- Inquire about their family members and recent happenings

Don't let the responsibilities and events of life keep you from sustaining relationships with your friends and family members.

Pearl

Keep Some Things to Yourself

S ocial media has created "snap-and-post" addicts: people who document every part of their lives by snapping pictures and then posting them to social media.

From live and unedited childbirths to home going services with pictures of deceased people in caskets, we've all seen videos or pictures posted on social media that would probably be better off being kept private. Simply put, everything is not for everybody. Everything that occurs in your life is not for everyone to know.

We all know people who are very active "posters" on social media. They document almost every moment of their life. They are constantly talking selfies and updating their statuses to inform the world about where they are, who they are with, what they are doing, and what they are wearing/eating/drinking almost every second of the day. You know what is going on in their life because they tell the world about it all of the time. It's almost like they can't actually enjoy the moment because they are preoccupied with photo-documenting it for the world to see.

One day, I bumped into someone that I had not seen in years. When we saw each other we both smiled, greeted one another, hugged, and had a general conversation complete with the "How are you doing?" and "How's the family?" questions. Afterwards, the young lady began commenting and asking me questions about a very personal situation. I was surprised that she knew about this issue! How did she know? I had not seen or spoken to her in years!

Well, as it turns out, she knew about this circumstance because I had posted about it! It was one of those posts I'd made in the heat of the moment, then deleted about 30 minutes after I'd calmed down. But she saw it, remembered it, and asked me about it! I made a decision right then and there that I didn't want people in my business like that so I wasn't going to make my business available for everyone to be in!

Your social media account is a type of brand in which you represent yourself and who you are. Everything that you say, do, post, re-post, and share represents your personality, your values, and what you stand for, and it will exist forever, even if you "delete" it. All someone has to do is screen-shot your post or picture and they will have forever captured evidence of your post.

Be mindful of going online to air your dirty laundry, your personal business, complaining about your supervisors, saying mean things because you are upset, etc. because it does not make you look good. At all.

Find a friend to talk to or take your issues to the Lord in prayer, but whatever you have to do, do not, under any circumstances, allow social media to be your personal garbage can.

Pearl

19

Unplug

At some point, we have all experienced life without our phones. Whether our phone was accidentally left behind, stolen or broken, it took a bit of adjustment to get used to not having our daily appendages and we usually can't wait to get them back.

Some people have trouble with managing their time because they are constantly checking their Facebook, Twitter, Snapchat, Kik, or Instagram accounts. We tend to waste a lot of time doing absolutely nothing from being busy scrolling on our phones and news feeds. Some of us notice the amount of time we waste and decide to go on social media or cell phone "breaks" for a period of time to help us "re-focus".

We have become a culture addicted to looking at digital media-so much so that people feel it necessary to occasionally announce that they are "fasting" from social media or deactivating their accounts. We have become addicted to the point where it is necessary to unplug. Take a break from watching television. Find something productive to do with your time as opposed to spending hours looking at your cell phone, tablet, and playing games. Instead, spend time enjoying the company of your loved ones, go for a stroll in the park, visit a museum, or even enjoy a movie. Life is full of colorful and entertaining options that can add liveliness and excitement to your everyday existence.

Contrary to popular opinion, it is in fact possible to live without social media and television. I will admit that having online access in the palm of your hand is indeed a convenience which allows you to remain connected to what's happening in the world. However, it becomes a problem when we can't go a few hours without checking our phones to get the latest updates from our "friends" and "followers".

One Sunday, my pastor was preaching on the importance of spending time with God, and he made the statement, "We all wonder why our lives are not where we desire them to be; why we don't have fulfillment and happiness within. We make time to look online but don't make time to read our Word. Instead of seeking Facebook, seek His face." At the time, this spoke volumes to me. It is very easy to mention how we don't have time to do certain things or complete certain tasks, but if you review the data usage in your phone, you can see that you have used four hours of data and 50% of your battery to browse Instagram.

I suggest implementing the following strategies to help you make better use of your time:

- Make a personal commitment to enjoying the people in your life. Put the phone away during dinner time, on dates, and when visiting family and friends.
- Cut your phone off at the same time every night and do not take it into your bedroom.
- Limit your time on social media in the same manner that you would limit television or video games for a young child.

Unplug. Put the phone and tablet down. Cut off the television. Pick up a book and read. Learn how to cook a new dish. Read a magazine to learn new makeup tips. Go to a park or outside for a walk or jog. Go visit a nature preserve. Get out from being stuck in front the screen and enjoy life and all that it has to offer.

Pearl

20 Be Open to Meeting New People, Going New Places, and Trying New Things

This Pearl is pretty straight forward: Do not limit yourself. To limit yourself means that you are not open to experiencing new things, thus you limit your experiences in life and stunt your growth personally, professionally, and spiritually.

At least once a month, make a conscious decision to visit someplace you have never been. This could include traveling to a different side of your city or even a new restaurant.

On our first date, my now-husband John and I met at an Ethiopian restaurant. It was a fairly new experience for us both. Despite his preference to eat at Longhorn, he remained open to trying Ethiopian dining. It was a unique visit. We learned that Ethiopians eat with their hands to form a connection to the food that they eat. They use rice or a bread called injera to scoop up their meats. I chose to eat with my hands but John wasn't going that far, so he chose to use a fork. Although I enjoyed the food, he did not particularly care for it, mainly because he was not used to the different spices and flavors that ethnic foods often contain. Ultimately, John enjoyed the overall experience. He wasn't particularly fond of the food but the overall experience broadened his horizons and provided us with a memory that we still reflect on to this day.

If you become open to conversing and speaking with different people, you will become amazed at the stories and experiences that lie behind a person's exterior. Sometimes we can be so judgmental based on assumptions we make about people, and our assumptions allow us to miss out on someone who could be a great friend or be a useful associate or connection down the line. Don't become so stuck in your own circle of friends that you fail to meet other people. Network and make connections. Converse with people and ask them questions about their passions, interest, and line of work. Maybe you could form some type of business relationship or collaboration, but you never know if you never talk to them.

Be open to traveling, going to new places, and try new things that will add to you as a person. In no way am I advising that you succumb to peer pressure or engage in activities that would be to your detriment. Make sure that your chosen activities add to you as a person and help to expand your mind and overall perspective. Ways to expand your network include:

- Attending networking events
- Joining interest groups on Facebook or Meetup and attending events
- Simply engaging in conversation with people
- Take an interest in others and engage in conversation as to who they are and what they do

Life is short. Do what you can, while you can, and enjoy yourself while doing it.

Epilogue

A natural pearl is formed when an irritant invades an oyster. The oyster then goes through a metamorphosis, and the end result is a beautiful, exquisite pearl. Oysters, soft and squishy, are not appeasing to the eye. However, after a period of transformation, they change into strong, beautiful and expensive gems. Oysters endure a tedious process to transform into pearls; therefore, pearls can be associated with great wisdom garnered through harsh experience.

As pearls are symbolic of love and purity, they are often used to embellish wedding gowns and also serve as family heirlooms, kept in families for generations as they are passed from grandmother to mother and from mother to daughter. Pearls are a traditional symbol of femininity and are timeless. They are rare and are associated with great value.

Proverbs 6:20-21 states in the New International Version, "My son, keep your father's command and do not forsake your mother's teaching. Bind them always on your heart; fasten them around your neck." Like a necklace of beautiful pearls, it is my prayer that you hold fast to the principles within this book and adorn yourself with them; fasten them around your neck. Share these pearls with your family members and friends in the same manner that pearls are passed down through generations of women.

Just like a pearl is rare and is associated with great value, know that you are rare. There is only one you walking on this planet. There is only one you with your appearance, your talents, and your purpose. Know that you are valuable.

Adorn yourself with these pearls and wear them proudly, confidently living a life of purpose on purpose as you walk in the glory who God created you to be.